Presenting Like a Pro
Mastering the Art of Public Speaking

Table of Contents

Chapter 1. Introduction

Welcome to "Presenting Like a Pro: Mastering the Art of Public Speaking" - a special report that's packed with charm, enthusiastic insight, and easily implementable techniques to make your public speaking journey both thrilling and effective. This guide, far from the complexities of a technical narrative, is an exciting ensemble of tips and tactics that will empower you to woo your audience and command the room with flair and finesse. Sprinkled with encouraging case studies of great speakers, insights from public speaking gurus, and step-by-step strategies, it's your must-have companion to master the art of self-expression in public. So, get ready to discover your inner orator, captivate your listeners, and make every speech an event to remember! Add this special report to your arsenal today and step on the stage with newfound confidence and eloquence!

Chapter 2. Unleashing Your Inner Orator: The Essentials of Public Speaking

Eloquence and confidence in public speaking are not inborn traits – they are acquired skills that you can master with practice and perseverance. This chapter aims to demystify public speaking, providing you invaluable insights and strategies for you to tap into your inherent potential.

2.1. Understand the Importance of Public Speaking

Communication is the backbone of our society. It allows us to form connections, influence decisions, and motivate change. It's not just about having something to say – it's also about saying it well. Public speaking, therefore, is a vital component of effective communication. Mastering it enhances your personal and professional life, expanding your influence circles and opening doors to opportunities.

2.2. Know Your Audience

The first step in any public speaking journey is understanding your audience. Knowing who you will be addressing can guide every aspect of your speech from formulation to delivery. Gauge their interest, their understanding of the matter, their demographic details, and their disposition towards you. This information will direct your tone, language, examples, and even your jokes.

2.3. Develop Your Public Speaking Skills

Like any other skill, public speaking requires continual practice for refinement. Start small, perhaps with a friendly audience, and gradually take on larger groups. Improvisational theater, joining a local debate club, or enrolling in a public speaking course can help sharpen your skills. Always remember – the more you practice, the better you become.

2.4. Harness Your Nerves

Public speaking anxiety is common even among seasoned orators. However, it's all about balance – while a little bit of nerves can keep you sharp, too much can undermine your performance. Practice techniques like deep breathing, meditation, and visualization to manage your nerves. Conducting dry runs, rehearsing in the venue, and reaching early for the event can also reduce your anxiety levels.

2.5. Master the Art of Non-Verbal Communication

Body language plays a vital role in how your message is perceived. From your posture, facial expression, and hand movements to your walk, everything communicates something to the audience. Learn to make eye contact, use gestures, mind your pace and volume, and project confidence in your stance. Remember, your body language should complement your words, not contradict them.

2.6. Attention to Detail

Crafting a great speech involves tending to every detail – from the opening line and structure to the appropriate and powerful use of language. Keep your purpose clear in your mind – whether its to persuade, inform, or entertain. Ensure you have a strong introduction to hook your audience, a body that skillfully presents your main points and evidence, and a compelling conclusion that leaves a lasting impact.

2.7. Use Visual Aids

Carefully designed visual aids can play a pivotal role in improving understanding, maintaining engagement, and adding persuasive power to your presentation. However, they should not dominate or distract from your speech. Your visual aids should be clear, relevant, and easy to understand.

2.8. Receive and Implement Feedback

Feedback is a goldmine. It can indicate which part of your speech was most effective or where improvement is needed. Welcome comments and criticisms from your listeners or mentors, and use it productively. Treat every speech as a learning experience.

2.9. Adopt a Growth Mindset

Public speaking, like other skills, grows better over time. Adopt a growth mindset – experience every stumble as a stepping stone towards improvement. It's essential not to view setbacks as failures but as opportunities to learn and grow.

Using these strategies, you can start on your journey to become a skilled public speaker. In the following sections, we will delve deeper into specific aspects of public speaking like use of language, story-telling techniques, humor, and managing Q&A sessions. Stay patient, stay prepared, and remember – it's not just about speaking well; It's about making your words count!

Chapter 3. Overcoming Stage Fright: Strategies for Staying Cool Under the Spotlight

"Stage fright—this pesky fiend can strike the most seasoned speakers who seemingly have everything else under control. But, there's good news. You can actually harness this nervous energy and transform it into a captivating and compelling performance. This section explores diverse strategies to help you keep your cool under the spotlight.

3.1. Understanding Stage Fright

Understanding stage fright is the first step towards conquering it. It's a common human experience fueled by adrenaline—the body's fight-or-flight response—that gets us ready for perceived 'dangers', in this case: public speaking. Symptoms feel physical: increased heartbeat, dry mouth, sweaty hands, or a shaky voice.

Researchers have found that stage fright isn't necessarily a sign of inadequacy. **The Charisma Myth** by Olivia Fox Cabane asserts that even wildly successful people like Warren Buffett and Sir Richard Branson have dealt with stage fright. They have not let this nervousness curtail their success but instead have found ways to channel it positively.

The most encouraging fact: stage fright is manageable and, with the strategies outlined below, we can learn to navigate through it successfully.

3.2. Embrace your Nervousness

Embrace the fact that the jitters you feel are not unordinary. Accept the emotions and aim to work with them, not against them. Evidence suggests that trying to calm down can backfire. Instead, channel anxious energy into excitement. This reframes the situation as a challenge, not a threat.

3.3. Practice Like a Pro

Nothing beats the fear as efficiently as practice does. Run-through your presentation multiple times, out loud, with everything you'll use on D-Day (slides, props, clickers). Practicing in a mirror or recording yourself can help identify areas to improve. Simulate the actual environment wherever possible by practicing on the exact stage or a similar venue.

3.4. Mindful Preparation

More than just about practising the script, it's crucial to anticipate potential pitfalls. What will you do if the mic fails or your presentation crashes? Having contingency plans will help you feel confident. Moreover, don't forget mundane yet essential tasks like checking the venue details (facilities, commute, parking etc.), ensuring your attire is comfortable and suitable, and packing any materials you need for the presentation.

3.5. Visualization and Affirmation

Visualization induces mental rehearsal to enhance performance. Mentally seeing yourself performing successfully not only boosts confidence but also reduces anxiety. Coupling this with positive affirmations (e.g., "I am a powerful speaker") implants self-belief. Remember to visualize the entire speech experience—not just nailing the presentation, but receiving the applause afterward.

3.6. Physical Warm-ups

Physical warm-ups, such as deep breathing or muscle relaxation exercises, can decrease symptoms of stress. Stretching, vocal exercises, and even power poses can get the body and the voice ready.

Also, something as simple as a good sleep the previous night and arriving early at the venue to familiarize with surroundings can work wonders in curbing stage fright.

3.7. Engage with your Audience

Seeing the audience as adversaries can only escalate fear. Engage directly with them; ask questions, share anecdotes, or encourage participation. When you build a rapport with them, they're no longer scary but rather co-participants in the conversation.

3.8. Giving your First Line a Headstart

A tricky moment during any presentation is its beginning. Consider memorizing the first few lines or using an attention-grabbing statement to make a strong start. The assured start boosts confidence, letting the rest of the speech flow more smoothly.

3.9. Reframing your Performance Thinking

Your presentation is not about proving your worth; it's about sharing valuable information. Shifting this mindset helps lessen pressure. You're serving the audience, not pleasing them. Still, if you fumble or make a mistake, remember that the audience is usually forgiving.

They empathize with you because most of them know what it's like to be in your shoes.

3.10. Adopting a Growth Mindset

Embodying the growth mindset—believing in your ability to improve with practice—can be incredibly powerful. Each speaking opportunity is a chance to learn, grow, and master the art. With every applause and critique, remember you're becoming a more learned speaker.

With these strategies in your toolkit, you'll find the stage less daunting. Remember: it's entirely normal to feel nervous before a presentation. With repeated exposure and healthy practice, you'll eventually perceive public speaking less as a threat and more as an exciting opportunity. Great speakers aren't great because of an absence of fear; instead, they have learned to use fear to their advantage."

NOTE Due to space limitations, this is a condensed version of what an exhaustive text covering 5 A4 pages would look like. For a longer piece, each subheading could be elaborated with more details, case studies, personal experiences, examples, and advice from experts.

Chapter 4. Planning and Preparation: The Blueprint of Persuasive Speech

Public speaking starts with comprehensive planning and meticulous preparation, forming the blueprint of your persuasive speech. Your objective here ought to be presenting a compelling narrative that informs, engages, and motivates your audience, turning passive listeners into active participants.

4.1. Understanding Your Audience

Study your audience, as this crucial first step is fundamental to shaping and tailoring your speech. An intriguing speech can flop if it doesn't resonate with your listeners, so focus on audience demographics, interests, values, and expectations. For example, if you are addressing a group of entrepreneurs, consider their business niches, problems they encounter, and areas where they seek growth and learning. Ask yourself:

- What are their expectations from the speech?
- What can they understand easily?
- How can you motivate them to act/feel/think differently?

Gather this data through pre-event surveys or interactions, which could be as simple as asking around, or as detailed as surveying attendants beforehand.

4.2. Clarifying Your Objective

Having a clear objective increases your speech's impact and guides your audience through the information you present. Are you aiming to enlighten, educate, persuade, or inspire? The objective of your speech will influence how you plan the content, structure, and presentation, so clarify it to provide your speech a clear path to follow.

4.3. Developing Your Content

There's no 'one size fits all' when it comes to content development. However, you can follow some robust principles:

- use simple and clear language, avoiding jargon and complex sentences. If you complicate the content, it confuses and disengages your audience.
- Use stories, anecdotes, and examples to make your points easy to grasp and remember, enhancing relatability.
- Vary the content to keep it interesting. Mix facts, stats, stories, interactive questions, and visuals to prevent monotony.
- Validate your arguments with related and reliable evidence.

Always have in mind that your speech needs to be valuable and exciting for the audience; otherwise, they won't connect with the content.

4.4. Structuring Your Speech

A well-structured speech helps your audience follow along, grasp complex concepts, and remember what you've discussed. Follow this typical speech structure:

1. Introduction: Ever heard the saying, "first impressions last"? Open with a short, engaging hook, clearly state your speech objective, and briefly outline what's to come.
2. Body: In this part, unpack your main points, one at a time. Each

point should be logically linked to the next for smooth transition. Use relevant examples or stories to support each point.

3. Conclusion: A great speech ends powerfully, summarizing the main points, reinforcing your objective, and offering a 'call-to-action'. This is your chance to encourage responses that align with your speech's objective.

4.5. Presenting with Presence

The delivery of your speech is just as critical as its content.

1. Voice modulation: Vary your speed, pitch, and tone for maximum impact.

2. Body language: Stand tall, make expressive gestures, and maintain eye contact.

3. Use of aids: Master your presentation tools to deliver an engaging visual experience.

4. Energy: Speak passionately to fully engage your audience.

4.6. Rehearsing Your Speech

You may think you know your speech inside out, but until you've rehearsed it multiple times, you learn there are unexpected stumbling blocks. How do your content and delivery work together? Are you within your allotted presentation time? Practice makes perfect, so rehearse until you feel comfortable and confident.

4.7. Gathering Feedback

Arrange a practice presentation with a small audience, preferably familiar and comfortable giving critiques. Feedback is instrumental; it can highlight where you could be losing the interest of your audience or spots where your transitions are not smooth. Make the necessary changes and... repeat!

Public speaking can be a daunting task, but with careful planning and preparation, you can give a persuasive speech confidently. Remember, speeches are about the audience, so always keep their interests at heart. Be clear about your objective, structure your speech well, deliver it with presence, and never underestimate the power of rehearsal and feedback. Take one step at a time, and in no time, you'll be on your way to captivating your audience like a pro!

Chapter 5. The Magic of Body Language: Speak without Saying a Word

Embodying the language of your body into your public speaking skills is not a simple task. It requires an understanding of how our bodies naturally convey information, how to control it consciously, and how to utilize it effectively during speeches. It's a language of its own that enhances the verbal messages you send and, quite often than not, have the innate ability of speaking louder than words.

5.1. The Natural and Unconscious Transmission

Human beings have evolved to communicate in many ways. Language is our most sophisticated form of communication, but we also convey meanings and messages through our actions, gestures, facial expressions, and body posture. These non-verbal forms of communication greatly impact how our messages are received by our audience.

In the realm of public speaking, verbal language is always complemented by body language. When a speaker remains stiff and ungainly, it introduces friction into otherwise seamless communication, tarnishing the innate charm of the spoken words. Conversely, a speaker who masters the art of body language can establish much deeper connections with their audience, making their narratives both engaging and compelling.

Notably, body language is a largely unconscious affair. We don't often think about how our body language is communicating to others. Yet, studies suggest that 55% of our communication takes place through non-verbal cues. Thus, the first step to mastering body language is understanding how our bodies naturally communicate and becoming aware of the messages we unconsciously send.

5.2. Calibration: Mastering Control Over Body Language

Control over body language becomes important as soon as we realize we aren't transmitting the signals we intend to. This awareness invites improvement, and improvement requires practice. It's just like learning any new skill—you start as a beginner, make mistakes, learn from them, and eventually become proficient.

Understand and learn the following key components of body language to incorporate them successfully into your public speaking skills:

EMBLEMS: These are body language symbols that have a direct verbal counterpart. For example, the peace sign has a clear meaning across various cultures. Using them adds a universal undertone to your speeches.

ILLUSTRATORS: These include the gestures that complement your verbal language and emphasize your message. For example, you might stretch your arms wide to indicate a vast amount.

REGULATORS: They help control, maintain, or signal levels of interaction and conversation between people.

ADAPTORS: These are behaviors that usually satisfy some physical or emotional need, like fidgeting or adjusting your tie when you're nervous.

AFFECT DISPLAYS: These involve facial expressions corresponding to the seven universal emotions: happiness, sadness, surprise, fear, disgust, anger, and contempt.

It's important to analyze your body language in various situations and strive for calibration—adjusting your gestures, posture, and expressions to improve their effectiveness.

5.3. Command the Stage: Body Language that Speaks Confidence

Good body language begins as soon as you walk onto the stage. Your posture must ooze confidence. The audience's first impression of you will be based largely on your walk and entrance—make it count. Maintain an upright posture, expand your body as opposed to crouching inward, and approach the podium with a confident stride.

Here are some extra tips using which you can sprinkle magic into your body language:

1. Maintain Eye Contact: Look at your audience. Make eye contact. This connection feeds back into your energy and stimulates a more vibrant, engaging delivery.

2. Smile and Use Facial Expressions: A smile speaks volumes. It conveys warmth, openness, and friendliness. Retain that and utilize other expressions in line with your verbal speech.

3. Use Gestures: Don't be a static speaker. Move across the stage when you can, use your arms and hands to illustrate points. Show enthusiasm. SHOW, don't just TELL.

4. Watch Your Pace: Slow down. Take deep breaths to calm your nerves. This will keep your body at ease and give you a more composed demeanor.

Mastering body language requires time, patience, and practice. But the payoff is enormous. By incorporating these strategies and techniques into your public speaking, you ensure your message isn't confined to words alone. Your entire being becomes an instrument of communication, making your speeches more passionate, compelling, and unforgettable.

5.4. Learn from the Pros: Analyzing Great Speakers

Great speakers have always used their body language to add dynamism and depth to their presentation, making their speeches memorable. For example, Steve Jobs, renowned for his presentation skills, was a master at synchronization between speech and body language. He used simple, natural gestures, open posture, great facial expression, and good pacing to augment his words.

Similarly, Martin Luther King Jr.'s "I Have a Dream" speech is marked by his charismatic use of body language to punctuate his message. His gestures matched his words, painting a powerful image for his audience.

You can learn immensely by observing and analyzing the body language of professional speakers. Notice how they move, use gestures, maintain eye contact, modulate their voices, and use facial expressions.

5.5. Practice and Review: The Path to Mastery

Mastering body language involves constant practice and review.

1. Practice in Front of a Mirror: Practicing speeches in front of a mirror allows you to see how you naturally convey yourself and identify areas for improvement.

2. Review Videos of Your Speeches: By recording your practice or actual speeches and reviewing them later, you can observe your body language in a more detached, objective manner.

3. Get Feedback: Encourage others to critique your use of body language. Friends, families, and colleagues can provide valuable feedback on your body language, often noticing things that you might not notice about yourself.

In conclusion, body language is crucial in public speaking. It not only accentuates your words but ensures your message resonates with your audience at a deeper, subconscious level. By mastering the magic of body language, you'll find yourself able to engage your audience like never before, turning public speaking from a task into an art. Remember, public speaking isn't just a task of expressing your thoughts but a comprehensive performance where your body is as much a part of the conversation as your words.

Chapter 6. Articulation Mastery: The Power of Pronunciation and Intonation

Having a clear and persuasive voice is essential for successful public speaking. Let's plunge into the fascinating world of pragmatic enunciation, pronunciation, intonation, and the strategic pacing of your words.

6.1. Understanding the Basics of Articulation

Articulation is the physical action of producing sounds, words, and phrases. As a public speaker, your objective should be to articulate your words clearly and effectively. All languages have phonetic and phonemic systems, and as a good public speaker, your effort should be to understand and master the systems of the language you use.

In mastering articulation, one must pay close attention to stress patterns, intonation contours, and the pace of speech. Speech, after all, is not just about stringing words together; it is about breathing life and meaning into words and conveying this through the intangible medium of sound. Dissect your sentences, practice them, record your voice and listen to it, identify your weak areas and work sincerely to improve those.

6.2. The Importance of Pronunciation

In the realm of public speaking, pronunciation is the key that can unlock numerous doors for you. Accurate pronunciation is essential for transmitting your message correctly and confidently. Mispronunciation can lead to misunderstandings and incorrect interpretations, potentially damaging your credibility and the integrity of your speech.

Invest time in actively improving your pronunciation. Using tools like pronunciation dictionaries, language apps, and even taking help from language coaches can greatly aid your journey. Besides this, make sure to also focus on accent reduction if it's causing obstacles in understanding.

6.3. Mastering the Intonation and Rhythm

While speaking, your voice naturally rises and falls, giving your speech a certain melody. This variation in pitch is called intonation, and it carries a significant chunk of your message.

Careful manipulation of intonation can change the meaning of a statement or how it's perceived. By laying stress on different words, you can shift focus, create emphasis, express doubt, convey surprise, and signify the completion of an idea.

Intonation is interwoven with rhythm. Rhythm in speech pertains to the duration of sounds in a sentence – how long should you hold a syllable or a silence? It's an essential component of delivery that, when mastered, can make your speech more engaging and effective. It offers your audience mental breaks, making it easier for them to process your message.

6.4. Implementing Articulatory Techniques

Now let's discuss some widely effective articulation techniques to improve your public speaking:

1. **Drills:** Have a set of pronunciation drills that you can practice daily. They can be tongue twisters, plosive exercises, or vocal warm-ups. Aim to articulate every syllable correctly and crisply.

2. **Mirror Practice:** Seeing how your mouth, lips, and tongue move when you speak can help you understand where a sound comes from and how to reproduce it accurately.

3. **Record and Replay:** Recording your speeches can help you detect issues with your articulation, pronunciation, rhythm, and intonation. Listen carefully to your recordings, assess your performance, look for instances of stutters, mumbles, rushed words, or mispronunciations, and devote time to improve.

4. **Hydration:** This might seem trivial but keeping your vocal cords hydrated can greatly enhance your speech delivery, preventing conditions like dry mouth which can hinder clear articulation.

5. **Breathing Techniques:** Proper breath control is crucial for good articulation. It affects the volume, pitch and quality of your voice. Practice breathing exercises to enhance lung capacity and control. Speaking should be as effortless as breathing!

6.5. Final Thought

Articulation mastery is a journey. As you begin to become more conscious of how you sound, you will naturally adjust your speaking techniques to improve. The best speakers are those who sound like they are speaking effortlessly. This does not come naturally; it is developed through consistent practice and a deep understanding of how our vocal machinery works.

Embrace the fact that your voice is as unique to you as your fingerprints. Sharpen it, nurture it, and learn to use it to your best abilities. Articulation mastery will open up countless opportunities for you as an empowering and effective public speaker.

Chapter 7. Audience Engagement: Crafting Speeches that Connect

The secret sauce to delivering a powerful speech is meaningful audience engagement. It's about crafting speeches that resonate, that ignite the collective consciousness of the audience, and impel them to respond - be it in thought, in feeling, or in action.

7.1. Understanding Your Audience

Understanding your audience is the first step in crafting a speech that connects. Whether your speech is intended to inform, persuade, or entertain, it will only prove effective if it resonates with your audience's interests, needs, and values.

Start by researching your audience. Who are they? What's their background? What interests them? What connects them? By finding the common threads that link your audience, you can weave a speech that resonates on a deeply personal level.

To get precise details, you can use surveys, interviews, social media, or direct conversations. These tools will give you a clear understanding of what your audience expects from your speech. For instance, an audience of business professionals might appreciate a presentation filled with data and facts, while a group of high school students might prefer a more engaging and interactive speech filled with anecdotes and visual aids.

7.2. Content That Resonates

Once you understand your audience's needs, interests, and values, you can begin crafting content that resonates. Every piece of information, every argument, every anecdote should have inherent relevance to your audience.

Strive for clarity, brevity, and specificity in your content. Avoid jargon and complicated language. The simpler and more precise your language, the more accessible and engaging it will be. Keep your content focused; it's easy for audiences to get lost or bored if you stray from the main topic.

Storytelling is a powerful tool to make content resonate. Comparisons, analogies, and case studies make your content relatable, bridging the gap between abstract concepts and real-world understanding. Stories humanize your content, making it more memorable and helping to foster a deeper emotional connection with your audience.

7.3. Using Interactive Techniques

Audience engagement is about more than just receiving information; it's about participation. Engaging your audience is about turning the traditional 'one-to-many' speaking approach into a 'many-to-many' conversation.

Incorporate interactive techniques to keep your audience engaged. These could include Q&A sessions, live polls, quizzes, group exercises, crowd-sourced opinion gathering, or even including audience input within the speech itself.

Remember, the more your audience participates, the more engrossed they are, the better they understand, and the longer they retain the information you're sharing.

7.4. Mastering Body Language

Non-verbal communication or body language can profoundly influence audience engagement. Good body language encourages trust, creates rapport, and enhances the overall charisma of a speaker.

Maintain good posture. Stand tall and steady on the stage, exuding confidence. Maintain regular eye contact with the audience to establish a personal connection. Use your hands to emphasize key points, which can improve understanding and retention. Also, use your facial expressions to add depth to your speech.

7.5. Fostering Environment for Feedback

The role of feedback cannot be over-emphasized in audience engagement. With feedback, you can be sure that your message is being communicated effectively.

Allow room for audience feedback during and after your speech. Engage in Q&A sessions and encourage comments. Listen openly to criticisms and use them as an opportunity for improvement. Take note of the reactions, both positive and negative, to your speech.

In essence, crafting speeches that connect is an art blending empathy, relevancy, interactivity, and non-verbal communication, all supported by a foundation of valuable feedback. Incorporate these elements in your public speaking endeavours to forge lasting connections with your audience.

7.6. Practice and More Practice

As with any skill, practicing your speech in advance can significantly enhance your performance. It helps in internalizing the content, reducing anxiety, and improving delivery. Consider recording yourself and watching it back. This will enable you to note areas for improvement, especially relating to bodily gestures, voice modulation, pace, and your use of pauses.

Crafting speeches that connect doesn't happen spontaneously. It is a careful, calculated process that requires thought, planning, practice, and a deep understanding of your audience. Invest the time and energy into mastering it, and you'll see your speeches move from mere presentations to powerful connections.

Chapter 8. Rhetorical Techniques: Tools for Impactful Delivery

In delivering a meaningful speech, the application of rhetorical techniques is vital. These tools, which can include the use of figures of speech, audience analysis, and persuasive strategies, play an integral role in making your message resound with impact.

8.1. Understanding Rhetoric

Rhetoric, in essence, enhances communication by influencing the perception of the listeners and effectively delivering the speaker's message. The art of persuasion, established by Aristotle, is encapsulated in three main elements: ethos (credibility), pathos (emotion), and logos (logic).

Ethos represents the speaker's character and credibility, shaping how the audience receives the speech. Pathos, on the other hand, stirs the emotions of the audience, creating a connection between the speaker and the listeners. Lastly, logos employs reason and evidence, offering a grounded and logical argument that appeals to the intellect of the audience.

These three pillars of persuasion, when used meticulously and in the right combination, can significantly enhance the impact of your speech.

8.2. Figures of Speech

Figures of speech are not just adequate for poetry, they can also add flavor and color to your speeches. A touch of creativity in your language can do wonders in captivating your audience's attention and making an impactful delivery.

1. **Simile**: This compares one thing with another using "like" or "as." For instance, "Words, when well chosen, are like 'precious gold'."

2. **Metaphor**: This asserts that one thing is something else, not in a literal sense, but in a comparative manner. For example, "Life is like a roller coaster ride."

3. **Hyperbole**: This involves exaggeration for emphasis or dramatic effect. For instance, "I've told you a million times already."

4. **Personification**: It gives objects or abstract ideas human characteristics or actions to add depth and dimension to your speech.

5. **Alliteration**: This repeats the same letter or sound at the beginning of closely connected words to create rhythm and emphasis, like "Peter Piper picked a peck of pickled peppers."

Remember, figures of speech can be a powerful tool in your arsenal, provided that they are used sparingly and appropriately, avoiding overuse or forced connections.

8.3. Mastering Speech Delivery Techniques

An impactful speech goes beyond the words written on a page. It leans heavily on the way these words are delivered. Here are a few techniques you could use:

1. **Pause**: A well-timed pause can create suspense, allow the audience to absorb your words, emphasize a point, or simply give you a moment to gather your thoughts.

2. **Volume**: Moderating your volume can help emphasize important points or evoke certain emotions. Loud volumes can show

excitement or importance, while a softer tone can convey sincerity or seriousness.

3. **Pitch**: Variation in pitch keeps listeners engaged. Monotones can be dreary and can risk losing the audiences' attention.

4. **Speed**: Speaking slowly can help emphasize a point, whereas quicker speech can convey excitement or urgency.

8.4. Storytelling: Touching Hearts, Changing Minds

Incorporating storytelling into your speeches is a wonderful way to connect emotionally with your audience. It fosters empathy and allows your listeners to see things from a different perspective. When crafting your narrative, consider your audience members, their experiences, and emotions, and shape your narrative that resonates with them.

Remember, the best stories have a clear structure – beginning, climax, and an end – and always reverberate with a strong message or lesson.

8.5. Pathos: Harnessing Emotions

Pathos primarily deals with the emotional appeal of your speech. This can be achieved by understanding your audience's feelings and values, and aligning them with your message. Storytelling, as discussed before, can be one of the effective techniques. Other methods can include invoking sympathy or anger, inspiring the audience, or appealing to their sense of identity.

8.6. Logos: Winning Arguments with Logic

Logos refers to using logic, facts, evidence, and reasoning to make your arguments more persuasive and credible. The key to this approach is to present your points in a structured, organized manner and support them with solid evidence.

The best speeches blend ethos, pathos, and logos seamlessly, taking the audience on a thought-provoking journey that is both emotionally stimulating and intellectually satisfying.

In conclusion, mastering these rhetorical techniques equips you with the skills necessary to deliver an impactful and unforgettable speech. Rhetoric, when used skillfully, connects you with your audience on a deeper level, making your message resonate with clarity and conviction.

Chapter 9. Storytelling Skills: Weaving Tales that Enlighten and Inspire

Everyone loves a good story. Whether it's an anecdote about overcoming adversity, a heartwrenching tale of loss, or a humorous escapade from the speaker's past, stories have the power to engage, enlighten, and inspire audiences. This chapter will delve into the art and craft of storytelling, providing you with easy-to-follow tactics and techniques to create compelling, relatable, and richly textured stories that your audience will remember long after your talk ends.

9.1. The Power of a Good Story

A story is not just an entertaining diversion. It's a powerful tool that can change hearts, minds, and ultimately, actions. Some stories make us laugh. Others move us to tears. But all of them awaken something within us—a curiosity, an empathy, a sense of shared human experience—that can convert passive listeners into active participants in your narrative.

So, what makes for a compelling story? The elements are straightforward: a relatable character faces a challenge, overcomes it—or doesn't—and changes as a result. However, crafting a story that successfully incorporates these elements is an art that you can master with time, patience, and practice.

9.2. The Structure of a Story

There's a science to the structure of stories. Across cultures, eras, and modes of narration, the most engaging stories often adhere to a three-act structure: the setup, the confrontation, and the resolution.

In public speaking, you can leverage this structure to create a narrative arc that resonates with your audience and amplifies your core message.

The setup introduces your story's central character and their status quo. In a public speaking context, that character is often you or another relatable figure. Remember, vulnerability can foster connection, so don't shy away from discussing failures, mistakes, or difficult circumstances.

The confrontation introduces the challenge, conflict, or problem that disrupts the status quo. This segment should evoke tension and pique your audience's interest, keeping them hooked as they wait to see the outcome.

Finally, the resolution provides the 'aha moment'—the point where the character solves the problem, overcomes the challenge, or otherwise learns or changes in a meaningful way. This is also where you make the point of your story crystal clear to your audience.

9.3. Crafting Your Narrative

Now, let's delve into how to weave your narrative:

1. Understand your audience: Knowing who you're speaking to can help you tailor your story's themes and messages for maximum resonance. Different demographics respond to different types of stories. What drives your audience—empathy? Curiosity? Ambition? Identify these drivers and use them to make your story more relevant and engaging.

2. Choose a relatable theme: Personal stories, real-life anecdotes, and tangible examples are more impactful than abstract concepts or data. Telling a personal story about a failure, for instance, would be more memorable and relatable than just saying "everyone fails sometimes".

3. Use descriptive language: Paint vivid pictures with your words. Don't simply relate events—describe them. Show, don't tell. Instead of saying "I was nervous", say "My heart was pounding like a drum".

4. Practice makes perfect: The more you practice your story, the smoother your delivery will be. Remember, even the best stories can fall flat with poor delivery. Practice your story until you can deliver it naturally, without hesitation, and with appropriate emotion and energy.

9.4. The Role of Body Language and Tone

Our bodies tell stories just as our words do. Our posture, gestures, facial expressions, and tone of voice can either support or undermine the stories we tell. Slouching, for instance, sends an unintentional message of disinterest, while a monotone voice can quickly bore your audience.

Therefore, you need to consciously use your body and voice to reinforce your story. Facial expressions should match the emotions you're describing, gestures should be broad and visible, your tone should fluctify based on the mood of your story.

9.5. Make Every Story a Lesson

Your story shouldn't just entertain—it should also educate. What can your audience learn from your story? The best stories are those that leave us a little wiser, a little more enlightened than before. This lesson doesn't need to be profound, complex, or earth-shattering, but it should be clear, on point, and beneficial to your audience.

To conclude, storytelling is an art that requires a synthesis of imagination, empathy, and self-awareness. With practice, you can harness its power to captivate your audiences and persuade them like no other technique can. The next time you stand before a crowd, don't just speak—tell a story. And watch your message come alive.

Chapter 10. Harnessing Visual Aids: Enhancing Your Presentation

The raw power of your words is important, no question about that, but if you can combine this with the power of visual aids, your presentation can go from humble to high impact in no time. Visual aids, when used correctly, can make your speech more engaging, understandable, and memorable. They bring your ideas to life, elucidate complex points, and bolster the emotions behind your message.

10.1. The Power of Visual Aids

Our brains are crafted in a way that visual information is processed much faster than text or spoken words. Visual aids can take forms as varied as charts, photographs, diagrams, video clips, infographics, and 3D models. They provide a break to the audience from perpetual listening and engage them in a different way, reinforcing your key points and insights.

10.2. Choosing Your Visual Aids Wisely

Like every tool in your presenter's arsenal, visual aids need to be thoughtfully selected and used. They should amplify your key points, not muddle or conflict with them. Always keep your audience in mind when selecting your aids – what will communicate your message most clearly to them?

When choosing your visual aids, consider the room's size where you'll be presenting. In a larger room, you may want bigger, clear aids that people can see from the back. In small rooms, more detailed aids may be more suitable. Also, keep in mind that a visually impaired person might be in your audience, so ensure the aids you choose are accessible. This may mean providing small individual aids or clear, audible descriptions alongside the visual ones.

10.3. Practical Techniques for Using Visual Aids

Once you've carefully selected the best visual aids for your speech, it's time to use them effectively. This requires clarity, confidence, and rehearsal. Here's how:

1. **Reveal only what's needed**: One paragraph or bullet point on a PowerPoint slide at a time keeps your audience in sync with you. This way, the audience doesn't read ahead and lose focus on what you're saying.

2. **Narrate clearly**: Any instructions or guides you give verbally should be done clearly and calmly. You can't assume everyone understands your aid on their own.

3. **Practice projecting and speaking with aids**: This brings coordination in your presentation. Failure to do so can create a disjointed, confusing presentation no matter how good the aids are.

4. **Use colors and designs consistently**: Color and design consistency aids recall and understanding while inconsistency can confuse your audience.

10.4. Incorporating Modern Technology into Your Visuals

It's the era of technology, and you can leverage it to make your presentation more engaging and memorable. Tools like Prezi and Canva can help you create better-than-ever infographics or presentations that can leave a lasting impression. You can even involve your audience using real-time polling tools, like Mentimeter, which allow them to interact with your presentation.

10.5. Case Study: Apple Keynote Presentations

Consider how Steve Jobs leveraged visual aids in his Apple keynote presentations. Instead of overwhelming text, Jobs used simple, clean, and high-quality images or a few crucial words pinpointing the core of his announcements. He would often bring physical products onstage to provide a tactile touch to his visual aids. The combination of imagery, words, physical objects, and Steve's undeniable charisma made his presentations unforgettable.

10.6. Final Thoughts

Visual aids are not a substitute for your words but a way to enhance them, to make them more engaging and understandable. To master the use of visual aids, consider your audience, context, and message. Practice beforehand and make sure everything blends together smoothly. Remember, when you captivate the eyes, you engage the mind, and the impact of your presentation thus escalates phenomenally. So, harness the power of visual aids for a presentation that hovers significantly above the ordinary!

Chapter 11. Pro Speaker Habits: Practical Tips for Continuous Improvement

A profound understanding of public speaking requires attention to detail, patience, and consistent practice. The words you utter represent you and echo your sentiments to the audience, and mastering speech delivery is key—but it won't happen overnight. This requires cultivating habits known to the proficient speakers who have tread the path before you. Let's embark on this explorative journey to unearth these habits and indefatigably guide your progression towards effective public speaking.

11.1. Speaking Is an Art: Start With the Essentials

One of the fundamental principles of successful public speaking is realizing and acknowledging its artistic nature. You're not merely stating facts or reading slides; you're narrating a story and stirring emotions. To do this effectively, you need to treat speaking as an art form, requiring several integral ingredients.

- Use a 'Schema': A schema provides a well-structured framework for your speech, helping to organize your thoughts logically and dramatically. It is similar to a stage play – having a beginning, middle, and an end. But this is not enough; focus on further embellishing these segments with stories, techniques and your personal insights.

- Practice makes Perfect: Absolute perfection might be unrealistic, but regular practice edges you closer. Treat every conversation as an opportunity to improve - the social gathering, the team meeting, or even the dinner-table chit chat. Every instance that you voice your thoughts moulds you into a better speaker.

- Seeking Feedback: Don't shy away from criticism. Seek constructive feedback from others and acknowledge your areas of improvement. Every remark that you receive is an opportunity to better yourself.

11.2. Break the Ice: Getting Rid of the Jitters

Nearly everyone gets jittery before a big presentation. The adrenaline rush and the jolting heart may seem petrifying, but they are your body's natural response to thrust you into high performance.

- Familiarize: Be aware of your speaking surroundings prior to the event. Speak to the audience during a coffee break, understand the venue layout, or perform a sound check. This will lessen any associated uncertainties.

- Breathe In, Breathe Out: Deep breathing curtails anxiety, psychologically preparing your body to calm down. This unwinding technique is known to decrease stress hormones, thereby increasing performance.

11.3. Your Audience is Your Best Friend: Establish the Connection

Remember, you're conversing, not reciting. Your audience is there to listen 'to' you and not 'from' you. Building this connection takes time and practice, but once accomplished, it amplifies the impact of your discourse.

- Engage: Ask questions, interact or maybe even tell a joke, ensure that you keep your audience engaged. Engagement builds a robust speaker-audience relationship facilitating a memorable exchange of ideas.

- Non-Verbal Communication: A warm smile, an excited nod, or an understanding eye-contact exudes your approachability. Likewise, active listening when the audience speaks makes them feel heard and valued.

11.4. The Buddha Within: Mastering the Art of Mindfulness

Public speaking isn't an outside-in process; it's inside-out. Nurturing your inner self forms the basis of being an effective speaker. Mindfulness – the art of being in the present, aids in fostering your inner peace and balance.

- Focus: Concentrate your energy on the current moment, on every word that you utter, and every reaction that you notice. This "in the moment" involvement aids in managing spontaneous responses and enhances your connection with the audience.

- Meditation: This ancient technique manifests mindfulness, which gradually turns into a lifestyle. A ten-minute meditation before your gig can work wonders in calming your nerves and collecting your thoughts.

The road to effective public speaking is incredibly enlightening and empowering. It paves the way for personal growth and professional recognition. Over time, you gradually sink into the shoes of a seasoned and charming speaker, but the journey is incessant. Remember, speakers are not produced in a day. They evolve and enrich their craft one day, one speech at a time. May this comprehensive guide accelerate your progression, nurturing you into the speaker that you always aspired to be. Embrace every word you utter, savor every moment you under the spotlight, and treasure every memory you create. Public speaking is an eternal journey, make it worth your while!